Export Import shipping solution

By

Joanne Campbell

Table of contents

Chapter 1 ....6 Steps to Starting an Import/Export Business

Chapter 2 ....Documentation for export and import?

Chapter 3 ....Frequently Asked Questions

Chapter 4 ....Summary

Chapter 1
6 Steps to Starting an Import/Export Business

Are you interested in starting an import/export business? Get everything rolling with tips from an effective business visionary.

Trade has existed almost as long as people have existed. In a more modern sense, imports and exports are how we can purchase nearly everything from around the world, including food, beverages, furniture, clothing, and the potato.

Any product or service brought in from one nation to another is an import, while products and services produced in the home nation are exported and sold to other markets. Therefore, your perspective on the transaction will determine whether you are importing or exporting a product—or both.

The cutting edge arrangement of worldwide exchange is a perplexing snare of import/trade organizations that handle the deal, circulation, and conveyance of merchandise starting with one country then onto the next. If you want to start a business in this field, you should know that there are many different kinds of import/export businesses. You could concentrate solely on exporting or importing. You could be a maker's delegate, work in a specific industry, or you could be an import/send out shipper or specialist, which is to a greater degree an independent merchant.

Starting an import/export business
There are a lot of things to think about if you want to start an import/export business, just like you would for any other business. A background in business,

international relations, or global finance is especially helpful for an import-export business. This ought to provide you with a comprehension of the bunch loops one should go through to sell or purchase an item from an abroad provider.

Selena Cuffe, co-founder of Heritage Link Brands, a company that imports, exports, and produces wine as well as other high-end products like tea and honey, asserts, "The compliances make it so complex that even if you did know how to do it, you're still going to have to keep in mind a lot of random considerations."

Before starting her own business in 2005, Cuffe held a number of trade-related positions and spent many years working in brand management for Procter & Gamble. She was inspired after going to the first Soweto Wine Festival in South Africa.

Heritage Link Brands now operates in a variety of ways within the wine industry: It exports grapes from its own South African vineyard to the United States, the Philippines, and

Hong Kong, in addition to importing wine from South Africa for the American wine market. Additionally, it exports wine for use on international flights to airlines.

Continue to peruse for the means you want to take to begin an import/send out business, as well as tips from Cuffe.

1. Get the basics of your business in order Anyone starting a business in the 21st century needs to cover certain bases, like creating a website and social media channels like Facebook and Twitter.

Therefore, here is your first step: Set the groundwork in order. This entails registering your company with the state where your headquarters will be, purchasing any necessary business licenses, registering a domain name, and so on.

Also required is a business plan. How to deal with the rules and regulations of the markets you want to work in should be covered in part of that business plan. For instance, you need a permit from the Alcohol and Tobacco Trade and Tax

Bureau, which is free but can take months to obtain, in order to import alcohol and tobacco products into the United States. Comparable exploration should be done while working with different nations, considering everything from different legitimate back name necessities in every country to protection.

Access to capital is probably your most important requirement. Startup expenses can fluctuate enormously contingent upon the kind of imports/sends out business you start.

According to Cuffe, "The first thing I recommend for anyone is to have your capital upfront." That is so you can shield your business from a legitimate stance as well as the value of the brand that you make and to ensure you put resources into the nature of anything that you send off. Test a market, a city, a state, and finally a region. Then, at that point, I feel that there are more noteworthy opportunities for progress and supportability long haul."

The amount of capital required to start a business comfortably (if one can ever be "comfortable" as an entrepreneur) and be prepared for anything that may occur, including issues with sourcing and changes in trade regulations, is demonstrated by the ratio that Cuffe cited as an example of success in the wine industry: "In order to make $1 million, you need to invest $7 million."

2. Choose a product to import or export The next step in starting an import/export business is selecting a product or industry that you are passionate about and believe could sell internationally.

For Cuffe, that item ended up being wine. She connected with the product not only in terms of taste and quality but also in terms of social justice.

"At the point when I previously entered the business in 2005, there was only one Dark winemaker and five Dark claimed brands," she says. " There are currently 31 Black-owned brands and 17 Black winemakers.

Cuffe claims that things have improved since the previous decade as a result of the increased sales and notoriety of South African wines worldwide, despite the fact that the South African wine industry still faces injustices such as unequal access to capital and poor working conditions.

The financing of Black businesses is our greatest accomplishment. At the point when we originally got everything rolling, for even these brands to make their own wine, they needed to source it from existing white wineries, since they claimed no land," Cuffe says.

After locating your product, you must also determine its target market. After all, you need to sell it to someone. Your ability to spot trends comes into play here. Products that are just starting to become popular or that show some promise of becoming so in the future are the best for an import/export business.

You can conduct research by using tools like GlobalEDGE's Market Potential Index or contacting local government officials and visiting websites like Data and Analysis maintained by the Department of

Commerce International Trade Administration. The Census Bureau of Foreign Trade also provides reports on the imports/exports industry's state.

From that point, it's ideal to begin "without rushing."

Cuffe tells you, "Test your ideas." Don't make the mistake of thinking that just because you like something, it will sell. What bursts into flames in the market is something other than the manner in which it tastes — it's who you know, and the bundling and good fortune of timing, and all of the aberrant delicate stuff that has the effect."

3. Find your suppliers Once you have a product that you want to sell internationally, you need to find a local manufacturer or other producer who can make your product and make a strong partnership with you. A decent connection with a provider is critical to long-running outcome in an imports/sends out business.

Suppliers typically can be found through platforms like Alibaba, Global Sources, and Thomas

Register. You should persuade the provider of the advantages of entering the U.S. market (or another market you wish to offer to), and sort out the coordinated factors of taking their item from their neighborhood stockroom or creation office to another, possibly on the opposite side of the globe.

You could also be your own supplier, as Cuffe sometimes is for herself.

"We own an interest in a grape plantation in South Africa called Silkbush," she says. " When I do business with them, I make it clear that 80% of the grapes we pick are sent to domestic wineries, where they are used to make their own exclusive high-end wine. The remaining twenty percent is used to produce our exclusive Silkbush label, which we export to foreign markets.

4. Price your product You have identified your target audience and the product with which you want to collaborate. The next step is deciding how much to charge.

Regularly, the plan of action on an imports/trades business incorporates two key understandings: the volume of units sold, and the commission made on that volume.

Make sure that the price of your product doesn't go above what a customer is willing to pay for it. This is called your markup, or commission. However, you shouldn't set it so low that you won't ever make a profit.

In the imports/trades industry, shippers and exporters normally take

10% to 15% markup above what the maker charges you when you purchase the crude item.

5. What's the next step in starting an imports/exports business? Finding clients to market to.

Finding customers is not the same as selecting a market. You cannot simply ship your goods to the Port of New York and begin selling them to anyone who passes by on the docks. Usually, you need to find customers and distributors who will take your product and sell it to other people.

Customers may find you if you have a high-quality website and digital marketing campaigns. Cuffe, on the other hand, suggests calling people cold to get things started. Contact the Chamber of Commerce in the area, trade consulates, embassies, and other local contacts, if you have any. These substances could possibly give you a neighborhood contact list that could be a fundamental assistance in beginning an imports/trades business.

I made a cold call to the Whole Foods store in Cambridge,

Massachusetts, and they gave me a chance. Cuffe adds, "Now we do regional and display programs with Whole Foods." Cold calls are still a big part of a lot of what I did in the beginning and still are.

6. Get the logistics in order The logistics of importing and exporting a product from one location to another and selling it is possibly the most complicated aspect. How does the product get from the South African vineyard to the wine glasses of Californians, for example?

According to Cuffe, "it requires an extraordinary amount of coordination when you are operating within a supply chain where your customer is different from your client, which is different from your consumer." I use a freight forwarder that contacts shipping lines like Maersk on my behalf.

Since they act as a transport agent for moving cargo, hiring a global freight forwarder is generally a good idea for all imports/exports businesses because it will save you a lot of time and worry about getting your products from the factory to a warehouse. Basically, you'll tell them about your business and what you want to do with the product. They'll arrange shipping, insurance, and sometimes licenses, permits, tariffs, and quotas for working in another country. Starting an imports/exports business in an international trade market can be a lot easier with this.

Chapter 2
What are documents for export and import?

The buyer and seller, as well as customs officials, carriers, and foreign governments, require important information contained in import and export documents. Fines and even the seizure of your goods by customs may result if you fail to include the appropriate documentation with your imports and exports.

When you start exporting and importing, certain products will

require particular documents.
Consequently, researching your
products prior to shipping is
essential.

Important Export Documents
When exporting goods, it is expected
of you to be familiar with numerous
documents. While some of the
documents are used to reveal specific
information about your goods,
others are unique to the export
process.

The following are typical export
documents to keep an eye out for:

1. Pro Forma Invoice The pro forma invoice is the first document you should be familiar with. A seller and a potential buyer typically use this document as a negotiating tool. A quote for a shipment of goods from your potential buyer is provided by the pro forma invoice.

A pro forma invoice can also include the following additional pieces of information:

• Specifications for the parties involved in the transaction—buyer and seller—goods description, appropriate HTS classification, price, terms of payment, and delivery details—cost, location, and method of delivery—currency used for the quote—in the end, pro forma will be used to generate the commercial invoice.

2. Business Receipt

The business receipt records data about the merchant of the products and the shipment. When the merchandise arrives at the purchaser, the business receipt can be utilized to review the shipment.

The government uses commercial invoices to verify the accuracy of all information and further assess customs duties. A government can specify the number of copies they require and request that the commercial invoice be written in a particular language.

3. Export Packing List In essence, export packing lists provide a list of the goods contained within the package or packages being shipped. Additionally, they specify the kind of shipping container that will be used for the goods. Some examples of packages might be:

• Drums

- Crates
- Boxes
- Containers

Packing lists are utilized for various purposes. For one's purposes, the two traditions authorities in the U.S. what's more, traditions authorities of the nation you're sending out to can utilize the rundown to distinguish products for examination. Second, export packing lists are used by freight forwarders to aid in the preparation of bills of lading.

4. Air Waybill All goods shipped by an international air carrier must have an air waybill. You will be able to keep track of your shipment as it travels thanks to the information that is included in the bill about the freight that you are shipping.

5. Bill of Lading Another necessary document for exporting goods is the bill of lading. The exporter and the shipper enter into a contract through the use of a bill of lading. Information regarding the shipment's type, quantity, and destination can be found on the bill of lading.

A bill of filling additionally works like a shipment receipt once the products are conveyed to their objective. Notwithstanding the items being sent and the method of transportation being utilized, a bill of filling must continuously be incorporated with a shipment.

Last but not least, the carrier, the shipper, and the receiver all need to sign the bills of lading.

6. Certificate of Conformity In most cases, certain nations demand certificates of conformity for

particular kinds of manufactured goods. A product's certificate of conformity demonstrates that it satisfies all requirements of both its home country and the destination nation.

The exporter is responsible for ensuring that the goods have been tested and meet the requirements of the certificate of conformity.

7. Declaration of Beginning
A few merchandise require a declaration of beginning, which is utilized by unfamiliar traditions organizations to guarantee that the

exporter in the nation of beginning follows levy guidelines. They can be generic, indicating that no trade agreements are involved, or a Free Trade Agreement certificate of origin, indicating that preferential treatment, such as free or reduced tariffs, may be granted. Both of these options are possible.

8. The government of the United States typically does not require export licenses. Around 95% of the products sent from the U.S. to different nations don't need a commodity permit. However, you might be required to have one in

other nations. Contingent upon the item you're sending out and the country you intend to commodity to, you might be expected to get a product permit.

Fundamental Import Reports

A few reports utilized for trading will likewise be utilized when you need to import merchandise. A few examples of these documents are a packing list, an airway bill, a commercial invoice, and a bill of lading. We will begin with documents that are unique to importing rather than repeating the information we provided for those documents.

These are the documents:

1. Bill of Passage
Bills of passage can be recorded by the shipper or by a traditional dealer chipping away at the sake of the merchant. Before your goods arrive, you must send this legal document. As part of the clearance procedure, officials from the customs department will conduct the necessary evaluations upon receipt of the goods.

2. Authentication of Protection

A protection authentication is a critical archive to incorporate when you import. Your goods' level of protection is shown on the certificate.

The insurance certificate will assist in determining whether insurance is included in the imported goods' sale price. The terms of the insurance coverage and instructions for what to do in the event that the import is lost or damaged will also be included on this certificate.

3. Even though it is not required, a letter of credit is a useful tool for importing goods. A letter of credit is a promise made by a buyer to a seller that they will be paid in full. Should the purchaser not have the option to take care of the expenses, then the bank of the purchaser will pay the sum extra.

4. License for Importation Customs and Border Protection (CBP) is the primary administrative body in charge of importing and exporting goods. To import, you do not need a license from CBP. However, when you import goods that are regulated

by other federal agencies, you may be required to have a license.

A few nations have limited products that you can't unreservedly import. Importing goods from these nations will necessitate a permit.

5. If your import is worth more than $2500, a customs bond will be required. There are two distinct options for customs bonds.

•A Customs Bond for Only One Use: A single-use customs bond will cover one import, just like its name suggests.

• A continuous customs bond: A persistent use customs bond will cover all imports made during a schedule year

For what reason Do I Really want Product and Import Records?

Whether you're a merchant, exporter or both, having the legitimate archives expected to send your merchandise is pivotal. First, when your goods enter a country, they must clear customs. Having the appropriate documentation will forestall any disasters like fines or capture of your merchandise.

For exports, getting your goods past customs is just as important. Additionally, numerous federal agencies in the United States monitor goods leaving the country. Additionally, you will need to ensure that your exports comply with the regulations of international customs authorities.

The shipping procedure is also made easier by import and export documents. Giving all data about the merchandise being transported

lays out straightforwardness
between the shipper and exporter.
Since face-to-face interactions are
uncommon in international trade,
this is especially useful.

Chapter 3
Frequently Asked Questions

Is it profitable to run an import/export business?

Numerous import/export businesses make a lot of money. To work on your organization's possibilities of benefit, it's critical to lead the necessary exploration on your industry and have a proven and factual strategy. It's also important to know your profit margins when pricing your products and all of the costs of running an imports/export business.

How do import/export businesses generate revenue?

As an import/send out organization, you'll create a gain by selling items at a higher rate than you paid for them from the merchant or source.

What is a license for exporting?

A product permit is an officially sanctioned record approving your organization to finish specific commodity exchanges. After the export transaction has been evaluated, the appropriate agency issues an export license.

I want to import goods. What paperwork do I need?

Depending on the nation into which you are importing the product, you will need different kinds of documentation to do so. While import licenses and permits may be required in the United States, an entry form from Customs and Border Protection is always required.

Chapter 4
Summary

The bottom line: Importing and exporting is a fascinating and intricate system that meets both emotional and financial needs. How can we get our hands on something that is grown or made in another part of the world? How can we ensure that those who produce and transport it maintain a sustainable lifestyle while simultaneously allowing others to enjoy it?

In the event that you're keen on responding to these inquiries, don't let the tremendousness of the undertaking overpower you. You can start your own successful imports/exports business with the right research, planning, and documentation.